Under Tainaron

Under Tainaron

a libretto by

Kelvin Corcoran

Shearsman Books

First published in the United Kingdom in 2025 by
Shearsman Books
P.O. Box 4239
Swindon
SN3 9FN

Shearsman Books Ltd Registered Office
30–31 St. James Place, Mangotsfield, Bristol BS16 9JB
(this address not for correspondence)

EU AUTHORISED REPRESENTATIVE:
Lightning Source France
1 Av. Johannes Gutenberg, 78310 Maurepas, France
Email: compliance@lightningsource.fr

www.shearsman.com

ISBN 978-1-83738-005-3

CONTENTS

SCENE 1

Cape Tainaron. The southernmost point of mainland Europe.

CHORUS OF ORPHANS

> They came out to us that night,
> ropes appeared and we climbed the cliffs,
> in darkness and roaring winds
> hauled up on ropes lowered by strangers.

ORPHEUS

> The sea brings in the news with morning
> and awake I found as if laid out to dry
> a torn inflatable, clothes, a rucksack,
> the nurse who went to Lesvos to help.

> The first decision determines all others
> the rest is rhetoric, advantage, ambition;
> and those stranded survive or die,
> the first decision determines all others.

EURYDICE

> She spoke about the camps
> about what could be done and not done
> the children who never saw the sea
> the mothers unable to talk.

> It's as simple as song
> to explain what happened on Kythera,
> the boats crashed on the rocks
> the refugees climbed the rocks to escape.

CHORUS OF ORPHANS

The locals came out to us that night
to help in darkness and high winds
lowering ropes from the cliffs,
to pull together in darkness and high winds.

The first decision determines all others
the rest is rhetoric, advantage, ambition;
and those strangers survive or die,
the first decision determines all others.

And your name Orpheus is our name,
as we rise and fall or drown in song
in the darkness of night, our name,
whispered along the migrant routes.

ORPHEUS

Yes, my name is your name
and we rise and fall in song,
though the world turns away,
my name is your name in song.

SCENE 2

Thresholds, broken doors, cave-mouths, collapsed houses,
sunken mineshafts in a destroyed landscape.

EURYDICE

I was there and then taken
into nothing, the chambered earth
from all I knew – nothing.

REFUGEE

A hole appeared in my life
the hole blown in my father's house
scattered me to the world.

E: I was there and then taken.
R: A hole appeared in my life.
E/R: On an ordinary day we fell.

E: Into nothing, the chambered earth.
R: The hole blown in my father's house.
E/R: Under the sound of the sea.

E: From all I knew – nothing.
R: Scattered me to the world.
E/R: Even our voices drowned.

EURYDICE REFUGEE

Nothing from nothing comes
the light consumes itself.
No speech can touch this zero

the ordinary day reversed.
We were there and then taken
deep deep this underwater silence.

SCENE 3

*Eurydice in the garden, a terrace above the sea backed by
mountains in a vast sky, Spring.*

EURYDICE

> Orpheus was special from the start
> neither village boy nor hired mouth
> he made the language sound
> across the wires of the world.
>
> Small sweet meadow green
> covered in April flowers
> beside the mountain track
> sings his big word to the sky.
>
> I made nothing of this
> but a platform of earth
> dressed in electricity
> of camomile, iris and vetch.

CHORUS OF SPOOKS

> Hades will eat this one up,
> send a messenger to gently lick,
> look how she drifts and smiles.
> Earth will open its mouth for her.

EURYDICE

> They say a god can just walk in,
> appear on an ordinary day

in a garden like this perhaps
and everything changes.

The music plays backwards then
as the light retreats and falters
even on a spring day
the roadsides flushed with green.

They say many things
and then there's nothing to say.

SPOOKS

Hades will fuck this one
enthrone her in darkness,
make her mute, compliant,
a sifting shadow death.

Genius of the earthquake zone
set the air a-tremble,
let the beasts out of their holes
to come and eat their fill.

EURYDICE

As if a woman all alive
could vanish in a garden,
in a flicker gone
turning to see the fountain.

A flicker at the ankle
just below that blue vein
in one still moment
exiting Spring and the light.

One day I walked in the garden
and was gone, the Earth opened
and darkness took me,
a flicker at the ankle and gone.

As if a woman all alive.
In one still moment.
Just below that blue vein.
Darkness took me.

SCENE 4

Entrance to the Underworld. Cape Tainaron, the Peloponnese.
Below the cape is a submarine cave entrance to the Underworld.

ORPHEUS

> I came to Cape Tainaron, the last of the land
> below the transparent doors of the sea hellmouth,
> the descent into only memory, into density,
> the sea near silent and no birds calling.
>
> A sea of boats, heading west, heading north
> and the boats were sinking full of people;
> and I noticed that children from the deserts
> could not swim and their mothers became speechless.
>
> To open doors of the sea, I came at night
> searching for Eurydice, the only woman;
> foundering dark descent into earthy roots,
> face down on the ground into only memory.
>
> So, I came to Cape Tainaron, the last of the land
> below the shifting doors into hellmouth.

CHORUS OF SPOOKS

> Do you know who we are slick boy?
> Do you know our names, do you know what we do?
> We're the Dark Ones at the Door, Sharp Ones at the Gate,
> Shadow Swallower, Eaters of the Thinking Meat.
>
> On the other side of seeing, we hold sway
> in the crowded darkness, you belong to us;

we can wrinkle the world in front of your eyes
spit you out like gristle, a knuckle bone, like nothing.

ORPHEUS

I know your names, I've always known them,
I walked the dark path of bloody roots
roots like shadows seeping deep entangled
roots underground, the light collapsed in stripes.

I know the earth gives way at every step,
foot sinks, birds stop singing; silence.
– My heart's a stone, I cannot speak,
I don't know what I'm doing.

Smashed down again and again,
face broken, head empty, staggering,
propelled into a wall of obsidian
I hit the mantle, fixed and dumb.

CHORUS OF SPOOKS

You Orpheus, orphan boy, flotsam
washed up on the common shore,
on the other side of seeing, we hold sway
in crowded darkness, you belong to us;

We can wrinkle the world in front of your eyes
spit you out like gristle, a knuckle bone, like nothing;
we're the triple word guards of Darktown
the captains of capacity – Send Them Back.

All the scattered of the Earth come here,
even you singer, Thracian pretty boy harping it;

go on Orpheus, move those rocks with song,
we'll show you how to Take Back Control.

Descend into the zero made of everything,
bloodless shadows sifting, smart mouth;
that's your wife, made transparent she rots apace,
see her hands hold nothing, she flits and stirs no air.

So, do you know who we are slick boy?
Do you know our names, do you know what we do?
Come on singer save her, take her hand, lead her home.
Sing it you fool, she's waiting, longing to return.

She rots apace, save her, take her hand,
say her name, take her hand, save her.

ORPHEUS

I know who you are and I'm unafraid
caught in the mineral density of loss;
deep katabasis to the core,
I slip into the shadow zone unafraid.

SCENE 5

The Immigration Removal Centre, Kent, at night.

CHORUS OF ORPHANS

> We are the children of the borders
> the liminal, the lost, the scattered
> who never made it across.
>
> The children of Orpheus,
> the dispossessed, the lost
> the internment camp caste.
>
> We are the children of the borders
> the liminal, the lost, the scattered
> who never made it across.
>
> Moths at the window tap a dark tattoo;
> the tunnels we entered we never left,
> moths at the window, children in the trees.
>
> Can you hear us now? Do you see us now?
> Children of the borders
> who never made it across.

ORPHEUS

> Choir of orphans sing louder still
> the world is deaf and turned away,
> sing the news in every channel
> tell the story of every route.
>
> Cross the Aegean to Lesvos
> march through Greece and Macedonia

sail the fatal sea to Lampedusa
scale the razor wired states of Europe.

Choir of orphans sing louder still
the world is deaf and turned away.
Choir of orphans sing louder still
the world deaf   turned away.

EURIDYCE

Come, stand there in the light.
you must sing your song, sing;
where we find ourselves there's only song,
come stand in the light and sing.

REFUGEE

That night   I was   driven   to a city,
I didn't   know   its name, no-one   told me.

EURIDYCE

Yes, that night, night of many nights,
you were driven to the city nameless . . .

REFUGEE

That night I was driven to a city,
I didn't know its name, no-one told me.
we were given a mattress, some food,
in the morning I could not speak.

The overnight journey to Tabriz
back of a Toyota into the hinterland,

we did the drop and walk in silence
walking around the checkpoints.

EURIDYCE

On dark tracks I walked
into another city unnamed
down down the airless descent
to see the faces of the dead.

EURIDYCE REFUGEE

On dark tracks, drop and walk
into another city unnamed
down into an airless basement
crowded faces of the dead.

Wait until night, think nothing,
make the deal with the agent,
there is a boat over the sea to Greece
and there is a tunnel back to Damascus.

REFUGEE

There is a boat over the sea to Greece,
there is a tunnel back to Damascus
there is a Centre on the coast in England
and there is a trapdoor you may stand on.

EURIDYCE

On dark tracks drop and walk
into the unnamed city of shades.

CHORUS OF ORPHANS

Moths at the window
children in the trees.
Can you hear us now?
Do you see us now?

Seascape, beach on Lesvos, littered with boats.

ORPHEUS

My still singing head
washed up on Lesvos
the singing head of Orpheus.

Amid the dead children
and other wreckage
a 25-minute crossing at $1,500.

My singing head proclaims
his name was Alan Kurdi
he was three years old.

Out of the arms of his mother
out of the arms of his father
they will never hold him again.

Out of the arms of his mother
out of the arms of his father
they will never smell him again.

Orpheus move the hearts of men
the mighty who know what they want
move the hearts of men who believe.

Orpheus who lost everything
singing truth from Lesvos
move the hearts of men.

His name was Alan Kurdi.
His name was Alan Kurdi.

SCENE 6

The Underworld.

EURIDYCE

> I walked into darkness eyes open,
> the ground at every step gone;
> I walked into darkness
> at every tread nothing stood.
>
> I walked into echo
> and then even echo died,
> drawn backwards into black zero
> and then even echo died.
>
> I walked into that darkness
> the light withdrew and ate itself
> and the sound was the sound
> at the end of waiting.
>
> The sound was the sound
> at the end of waiting
> and then even echo died
> and then . . . .

ORPHEUS

> Must not speak
> walk she follows
> don't look back
> must not speak.
>
> You rid he see
> you you you rid

rid he he he
see sea see seed

Eurydice Eurydice Eurydice

EURIDYCE

(*Not seeing or hearing Orpheus.*)

I thought there was a sound,
the sound at the end of waiting
but no and then even echo dies,
I only fall, only fade, no-one there.

ORPHEUS

How can I not speak your name?
All is lost in that moment of song,
your name set half of hell spinning.

I beg you Hades, I beg you
let me take back but a few steps,
draw back that spoken name.

Eurydice Eurydice Eurydice

(*Eurydice begins to fade backwards from sight.*)

Then turning and saying
her hand on my shoulder
its warmth lighter than – gone
and then turning, gone.

EURIDYCE

I thought there was but no,
my hand rests on nothing now
I am nothing now.

I thought there was a name
Or? phe? us? Or? phe? us?
but no, there's no echo now.

My hand rests on nothing.
I thought I heard but only air.
No name. N on ame. Em anon.

orph ph ph pr ho su us ee oro ep he eu eu

ORPHEUS
(Singing to the empty air.)

Did you think I could let you go so easily
or return a shade with nothing to say?
I saw none of this from above,
only the empty garden, the broken ground.

But I would see you leaning over me,
your dark hair, your eyes stare down burning
the first night we spent ourselves on each other,
I would see you leaning over me.

I would always want to touch you again
to know what you are wearing, touch your face,
if I could assemble the shadows and light
which lie in the folds of your discarded clothes.

SCENE 7

Outside the Home Office of Darktown.
The Home Secretary speaks impromptu.

THE HOME SECRETARY

Yes, we know the objections you've raised,
wind from the distant world sifts our borders
but there's no revelation here
just a capacity question – and small boats.

We have determined that refugees should drown
I mean children and their parents;
the mechanisms of drowning are complex,
skin cooling, amnesia, fibrillation etc

We all know the English Channel is chilly,
it ranges between 20 and 5 degrees
and yes, of course, in water below 28
the heart may stop spontaneously.

How long it takes to drown varies,
consider body size and fat insulation,
immersion at 5 degrees can result
in drowning between 30 to 60 minutes.

A small child would drown sooner,
in that narrow band of water
tightened to choke the nation.
OK. Are there any more questions?

GHOST EURIDYCE

> Minister – will you stand in this pool of light?
> Only where there's song, we find ourselves.
> Will you raise a little aria from the streets of Darktown?
> Will you come stand in this pool of light?
>
> We need a little aria of the ordinary world
> to recall lighted windows, crowded rooms
> to spin us through these temporary days
> before the sea was a trapdoor and we fell.

THE HOME SECRETARY

> Well, if there are no more questions?

GHOST EURYDICE

> The sea made us dance in an arc
> but not the village square circle, as if
> turning an oar, a body, a head
> in the basin of the blood-dark sea.
>
> I am crouching ready to jump
> I am dancing with my family
> I am possessed by that music,
> like the boat, around us then nowhere.

HOME SECRETARY

> OK? Let's wind it up then.

GHOST EURYDICE

We threw everything overboard
and a music filled our mouths
and that music was lamentation *furens*
and some were suspended in watery space.

If I could picture what happened,
the sea's slow unpicking and dismemberment,
I would make this picture to tell you
and words in the water did not save us.

HOME SECRETARY

OK then.

GHOST EURYDICE

Minister, will you lay that body down?
Small enough for one pair of hands.
Small enough for your hands to carry?
Will you lay that body down?

CHORUS OF ORPHANS

Moths at the window
children in the trees.
Can you hear us now?
Do you see us now?

SCENE 8

The Underworld

ORPHEUS and EURYDICE

> I was there and then taken
> into nothing, the chambered earth
> from all I knew nothing.

ORPHEUS AND EURYDICE

> E: Into nothing, the chambered earth.
> O: I turned and spoke your name.
>
> E: From all I knew nothing came.
> O: You fell away into darkness.

ORPHEUS

> Did you think I could let you go so easily
> or return a shade with nothing to say?
> I didn't see any of this from above,
> only the empty garden and broken ground.
>
> But I would see you leaning over me,
> your dark hair, your eyes stare down burning
> the first night we spent ourselves on each other,
> I would see you leaning over me.

EURYDICE

> And I would see you leaning over me,
> your dark hair, your eyes stare down burning

that first night we turned the days inside out
I would see you leaning over me.

I would always want to touch you again,
to know what you are wearing, touch your face;
there's nothing for me there if not you,
the days turning and turning in our hands.

ORPHEUS

I would always want to touch you again
to know what you are wearing, touch your face
if I could assemble the shadows and light
which lie in the folds of your discarded clothes.

ORPHEUS and EURYDICE

They would speak the life we hold in our hands,
show the shape we know and slow the running film.
If I were a lark and could rise to sing
I would speak those words and slow the running film.

SCENE 9

Cape Tainaron

ORPHEUS

> The first decision determines all others
> the rest is rhetoric, advantage, ambition;
> and those strangers survive or die,
> the first decision determines all others.
>
> The sea brings in the news with morning
> and awake I found as if laid out to dry
> a torn inflatable, clothes, a rucksack,
> the nurse who went to Lesvos to help.

EURYDICE

> She spoke about the camps
> about what could be done and not done
> the children who never saw the sea
> the mothers unable to talk.
>
> It's as simple as song
> to explain what happened on Kythera,
> the boats crashed on the rocks
> the refugees climbed the rocks to escape.

CHORUS OF ORPHANS

> The locals came out to us that night
> to help in darkness and high winds
> lowering ropes from the cliffs,
> to pull together in darkness and high winds.

The first decision determines all others
the rest is rhetoric, advantage, ambition;
and those stranded survive or die,
the first decision determines all others.

They came out to us that night,
ropes appeared and we climbed the cliffs,
in darkness and roaring winds
hauled up on ropes lowered by strangers.

And your name Orpheus is our name,
as we rise and fall or drown in song
in the darkness of night, our name,
whispered along the migrant routes.

ORPHEUS

Yes, my name is your name
and we rise and fall in song,
though the world turns away,
my name is your name in song.

AFTERWORD

My thanks go to Jack Hues for his advice and support in my tentative first steps with this work. Parts of *Under Tainaron* are recast from poems already written and published over several years. As a libretto it only lacks music. Cape Tainaron, Cape Matapan, is the southern point of the Mani peninsula and the southernmost tip of mainland Europe. The submarine cave entrance into the underworld is below the cape. Mythology tells us this is where Orpheus ventured in his failed attempt to rescue Eurydice. The name Orpheus and the word orphan are cognates.

www.ingramcontent.com/pod-product-compliance
Lightning Source LLC
Chambersburg PA
CBHW021948040426
42448CB00008B/1298